BYGONE I

IN NORTH WALES
& SNOWDONIA

The first sod of a railway connecting Llanberis the with summit of Snowdon was turned on December 15th 1894. On January 8th 1896, a passenger train ran to the summit. The line has a guage of 2ft 7½ and is 4.75 miles long (nearly 8km). The gradient is no steeper than 1:5½ (18.2%). This detailed image portrays visitors at the summit

Helen Maurice-Jones

Landmark Publishing

Published by

Landmark Publishing

The Oaks, Moor Farm Road West, Ashbourne, DE6 1HD
Tel: (01335) 347349 Fax: (01335) 347303
Email: landmark@clara.net Web: www.landmarkpublishing.co.uk

1st Edition

ISBN: 978-1-84306-414-5

Printed by: TJ International, Cornwall

Design: Mark Titterton

Front cover: Rossett Station, with many farmers waiting to load their milk churns. This was a busy station in its
heyday as the station was on the line from Shrewsbury to Birkenhead via Chester

Back cover Top: The Ffestiniog to Bala train leaving Blaenau Ffestiniog in 1883, the year the branch line was opened
by the Great Western Railway **Back cover bottom-left:** Shop fronts in Bangor. Taken in the early 1920s, Bangor

Back cover bottom-right: Felin Isaf, at Bryndu, Rhosneigr, in its working days

Opposite: Menai Bridge. Until a major restructuring of the supports for the bridge-deck in the 1930s, there were
four sets of supporting chains, shown here. The outside original chains were replaced with lighter but stronger steel
chains, which allowed the removal of the middle two sets and a heavier load of traffic. The original chains were made
up from 33,264 flat iron bars made at Upton Magna, near Shrewsbury

BYGONE DAYS
IN NORTH WALES
& SNOWDONIA

Helen Maurice-Jones

Landmark Publishing

An early view of the White Lion Inn and the parish church at Llanelian. Investigations are being undertaken to try and show that the inn potentially could be one of the oldest in Wales

A popular tourist route was the road up the west flank of Snowdon, from Beddgelert to Caernarfon. It went passed the Snowdon Ranger Hotel, a popular stopping place and starting point for one of the routes up Snowdon. It is now Snowdon Ranger Youth Hostel

INTRODUCTION

This book brings together a selection of photographs, many from the early part of the 20th century and some even earlier. It will take you, the reader, on a journey through North Wales reproducing a lovely collection of scenes of yesteryear. For some, it may evoke nostalgia and for the younger reader, a fascinating insight to a time long gone, although many places have of course remained unchanged.

These images depict a time when the pace was slower, roads were often narrow and uneven; and transportation by rail and sea was much more common. A good example of this was the movement of slates from Blaenau Ffestiniog, which involved the use of both the Ffestiniog Railway and shipping from the quayside at Porthmadog. Other examples of this were common in the region.

Weekly markets and annual or statute fairs were a social event, illustrated in the photographs of Llanrwst, Corwen and Dolgellau. Whilst the popularity of Llandudno remains unchanged as a holiday destination, the scenes on The Promenade and the beach are unfamiliar these days. We now longer have bathing machines or ships bringing visitors by sea to the pier.

Also included in my selection are images of buildings now lost or altered, such as an old water mill at Betws-y-coed; The Victoria Hotel at Llanrwst and The Pavilion at Rhyl. I hope the book succeeds in portraying a more tranquil, different way of life and that every turn of the page is an enjoyable experience.

I wish to thank the Record Office, Ruthin and Pat Peckham for the use of photographs.

Helen Maurice-Jones
September 2008

Above: The Snowdon
Mountain Railway
with a train near to the
summit

Left: An early view
of the Victoria Hotel,
Llanberis. It is situated
opposite the Snowdon
train station

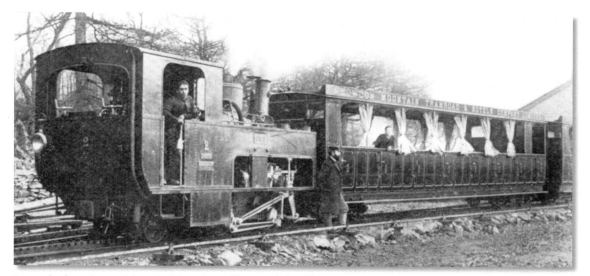

It may look antiquated, but the Victorian rolling stock is still in use today and is a major feature of the Snowdon railway. Notice the curtains of this open sided coach

A group of passengers await boarding of the train

Two views of Llanberis, looking south (above) and looking north (below)

A drover with a flock of sheep heading away from Llanberis

A horse drawn vehicle on the Llanberis Pass

Two lovely views of Caernarfon castle in the days when sailing ships could be
regularly found tied up by the castle

This scene in Caernarfon shows one of the town gateways which was converted into the guildhall, with a pleasing result. This building was formerly the east gate of the town

Another view of the gate and Eastgate Street

Strolling by the town wall, with the Eagle Tower in the background and the River Seiont on the right

An interior view of Caernarfon Castle looking towards the Eagle Tower, clearly showing a well preserved cannon. Caernarfon Castle is a magnificent example of a feudal fort and is rivaled by few other castles in the country

Caernarfon's Square was the venue for fairs and large gatherings, surrounded by a few principal buildings, such as the Post Office, banks and the Presbyterian Church. A monument to Sir Hugh Owen, who spent his life furthering the educational interests of the Principality and a fine bronze statue of the great Welsh Prime Minister, David Lloyd George, have been erected here

This scene of one of the finest bridges in the Principality (Britannia Bridge) no longer exists and even if it did, tree growth prevents the scene from being repeated. Built in 1850 by Robert Stephenson, it was badly damaged by fire in 1970. The opportunity was taken to build a road link across the bridge as well as the railway and this is now the main road bridge to Anglesey. The two lions guarding the western end of the bridge seen here remain but are at the railway level and are therefore missed by motorists. Also missed by most people is the statue of Nelson, which exists at the side of the Menai Strait just off the right side of this view. It commemorates not just a national hero but many Welsh sailors who contributed to the victorious campaign which culminated in the Battle of Trafalgar, 1805. Construction of the original bridge began in 1846 and took four years to complete, costing £602,000

Menai Bridge built between July 1818 and July 1825. It was offically opened on 30th January 1826. It cost £120,000 to build and a further £26,577 was paid to five redundant ferry companies. The bridge is 560ft long and the chains were initially each 1,715 feet long, with the bridge deck 100ft above the river. It had to be this high to allow sailing ships to clear their masts. The first cart to use the bridge belonged to the Amlwch Brewery Co. See also p3

A lovely view of tranquility in the middle of Menai Bridge village

A steamer unloading passengers at Menai Bridge pier

The ladies in the foreground of the scene at Beaumaris castle give some idea of the age of the photograph. The fortress was built in c. 1280 by Edward I and the ivy-clad ruin was as popular with visitors in Edwardian and Victorian days as it is now

A peaceful view of Beaumaris looking out over the Menai Strait with the pier in the distance. Steamers used to stop at the pier to pick up and land passengers

Beaumaris from the pier

Penmon Priory is situated a few miles from Beaumaris. It dates from the 13th century

Left: Llangefni showing Bulkeley Square and the Bull Hotel

Right: The High Street in Llangefni

Left: Felin Isaf, at Bryndu, Rhosneigr, in its working days

The *R.M.S. Munster* steaming past the lighthouse at Holyhead

The London and North Western Railway Station and Harbour at Holyhead with two ferry boats

This was the most direct route to reach Beaumaris from Bangor. Steamship ferries would leave Garth Pier daily in the season (costing 6d/2.5p in 1912). A steamboat also left this pier to reach Caernarfon on the Menai Strait, also stopping at Menai Bridge. This pleasant sea journey gave fine views of Snowdonia as well as Anglesey

The view looking over Bangor towards Beaumaris

Messrs Jones Bros., Bangor Ltd, Automobile Engineers. This garage was situated in High Street and was advertised as being distributors of 'Buick, Oldsmobile and Chevrolet cars, also GM trucks, Morris Cowley and Morris Oxford cars'. The advert also states that there were competent engineers, electricians and coach builders in attendance, 'prepared for any mishap'. They were also stockists of a fine selection of Marconi wireless sets!

The gates of Penrhyn Castle were a popular stopping place for different forms of transport bringing many visitors to the area. In the early 20th century, when this photograph was taken, the castle was open to visitors on Tuesdays and Thursdays.

A selection of views of old shop fronts and a shop interior in Bangor. Taken in the early 1920s, at that time, Bangor had 12,000 inhabitants. The older part of the city was the business quarter and was in the Valley

This shows the old road, weaving its way from Bethesda towards Llyn Ogwen and Tryfan. This route was popular early in the 20th century and was used by daily coach tours from Colwyn Bay, departing at 10am prompt, changing horses at Betws-y-coed and again at Bethesda. The tour returned at 6.30pm and cost 10 shillings (50p) plus an extra 2 shillings (10p) for a box seat

Penmaenmawr from the east. In 1923, the air around here was described as pure and salubrious, breezing in from The Irish Sea, whilst invigorating and bracing when rushing down from the mountains

The railway from Chester to Holyhead passes through a tunnel at Penmaenmawr. The railway separates the houses from the sea (as it does at Colwyn Bay). However despite this, the town combined the advantages of sea and mountains and with easy access provided by the railway, its position helped create the town's popularity

Below: This view clearly shows the pier from which local stone of commercial value was loaded and transported on ships. The expanse of beach, still popular with visitors, was very much a place for bathers and in the early 20th century, the authorities spent £20,000 on the construction of a promenade for the many visitors

An early photograph of the main street depicting a very sedentary pace of life. Described over a century ago as a quiet seaside resort in a fertile valley. It is overshadowed by a massive headland, which gave the town its name: 'head of the great rock'. Penmaenmawr was frequented by WE Gladstone and Mrs Gladstone retired here after his death

Visitors enjoying the beach at Penmaenmawr

The Parade at Llanfairfechan (top) and the beach (below)

There can be few approaches to a town in the UK which commands such an impressive sight as that approaching Conwy from Llandudno Junction. This most impressive of Edwardian castles was built for Edward I in 1284. It is built on walls 15ft thick and with only two ways of entry – from the river and via a former drawbridge at the top of Castle Street

The Conwy suspension bridge, seen here from the castle, was built in 1822-26 by Thomas Telford. A footway for the benefit of pedestrians was added between the road and the railway bridges in 1904 and was known as the Water Bridge, but this has now been removed. The tubular railway bridge was begun in 1846, the same year as the Britannia Bridge over the Menai Strait, and opened in 1848

Two views of Conwy Castle interior showing surviving arches of The Great Hall. Two of the arches subsequently fell and regrettably have not been put back

The Uppergate Street Arch (Porth Ucha) from inside the Conwy town wall. Beyond the arch is part of 'The College'

The Lowergate Arch Conwy, adjacent to the Liverpool Arms and the quayside (the R'odyn)

Above and right: The boats of the fishermen and mussel fishers on the River Conwy. Still commercially important, the industry is smaller than it used to be. A pearl found in one of the mussels was presented to Catherine, wife of Charles II and is said to be in one of the Royal Crowns to this day (they married in 1662)

Conwy pier was used by the regular river traffic carrying visitors to Tal-y-Cafn and Trefriw

Left: The Bangor Road Arch, Conwy, which was built to allow Telford's road to Bangor to leave on a new alignment. The arch was inserted into an existing tower

Below: A very old view of the Conwy town wall, apparently prior to any buildings being erected adjacent to the walls

Left: This tower was part of the The College and was situated just above the Uppergate Street Arch which is visible behind. This photograph, together with the previous one and the one below are thought to be of 19th century date

Below: An early photograph of Conwy station. It opened in 1848 following the completion of Stephenson's tubular bridge over the river. The town wall had to be breached to allow the railway to enter the town (as seen here) and the bridgework incorporated copies of the castle towers

Conwy town from the south before much development had taken place in this area

Above and right: This lovely half-timbered building in Conwy was once a temperance hotel, sometimes described as one of the oldest houses in Wales. Known as Aberconwy House, it was also a coffee tavern for a while. It is now owned by the National Trust and is open to visitors

The flannel mills of Thomas Williams and Son at Trefriw. A water-driven fulling mill was established here in the 19th century. It was bought by Thomas Williams in 1859. Cloth from the hand looms was washed, finished and dried and then stretched in a nearby field

This view shows the shops in Trefriw and the former Gerionydd Hotel, now the Fairy Falls Hotel. By 1910, Trefriw had become a leading social centre in the summer months. The Edwardians enjoyed facilities and functions provided by the Trefriw Improvement Company and of course, the nearby spa

Early visitors to the Trefriw Spa. It has remained a tourist attraction to the north of Trefriw

The slate quay at Trefriw in 1857. This scene is believed to have been taken by the well known photographer, Roger Fenton. There has been a quay at Trefriw for centuries. Large ships have docked here since Roman times, followed by medieval and later traders. At one time, 42 tons of Dolwyddelan slates were shipped regularly from here to New Orleans

Another view of the landing stage at Trefriw, some 10 miles (17km) from the sea. Paddle steamers were the last ships to ply the river and used to make trips from Conwy, Deganwy and Llandudno, regularly going as far as the quay at Trefriw. These stopped in 1939 and were not reinstated after the War

Disembarking passengers at Trefriw with the *PS King George* nearest the camera

The Trefriw spa was very popular with the Victorians who came to take the waters. It lost all of its visitors with the outbreak of the Great War in 1914. The trade has been revived and the spa is very popular again

A pony and trap taking guests from the paddle steamer to nearby attractions at Trefriw

Tal-y-Cafn sits on what may well be one of the oldest trading routes in Western Europe, being on a prehistoric route way. It was an ancient crossing when the Romans established a fort nearby. It was here that later drovers swam their animals across the river at low tide and an inn existed on the west side of the crossing (see above) along with a compound to corral the animals until the next low tide. The crossing was made much easier by the bridge, which was built in 1897

Two views of the bridge at Tal-y-Cafn

The Bridge, " Tal-y-Cafn ".

Gower's bridge in Edwardian times. This was built to link the spa at Trefriw with the railway station at Llanrwst. It was a timber trestle bridge used by horse drawn carriages

The Victoria Hotel, Llanrwst (now demolished) and the bridge, looking upriver. The town was an important crossing point of the River Conwy, being the lowest bridge until the Conwy suspension bridge was built

Two views of the Victoria Hotel

Left: The view from the hotel was similar to this view, i.e. over the bridge to Tu-hwnt-i'r-bont and Gwydr Avenue

The Cattle fair on a rainy day in Denbigh Street, Llanrwst. It was common for fairs to spill out into neighbouring streets. Because of the bridge, Llanrwst was a gathering place for drovers who brought their herds of Welsh Black Cattle here on the first leg of their journey to English markets, travelling as far away as the important Barnet Fair. Other drovers used to swim their animals over the river at Tal-y-Cafn

The Market Place in Llanrwst has been the focal point of trade in this section of the Conwy Valley for hundreds of years. As far back as 1328 it was compulsory to publish the date when a market or fair was held. In 1830, there were eight fairs being held here

Market day in Edwardian times in Llanrwst

A tranquil scene in Station Road, Llanrwst. Note the gas lamp on the left hand side

This view is of Pont-y-Pair, an old stone bridge over the River Llugwy at Bettws-y-coed. Sharp pointed rocks and boulders in the bed of the river make it particularly interesting to artists and photographers

Waterloo Bridge at Betws-y-coed, celebrating the battle of 1815, when Telford's bridge was completed

Right: This former mill was at Bettys-y-coed according to the original photograph

Below: The main street of Bettws-y-coed with a horse waiting patiently outside the shop on the left. You would be hard pressed to find the village this quiet today

The Miner's Bridge, is situated on the Capel Curig side of Betws-y-coed, originally constructed for the benefit of miners working north of the river. It has long been a popular tourist attraction as can be seen from this photograph

The view over Capel Curig, Llynnau Mymbyr and Dyffrin Mymbyr towards the Snowdon range, taken about a century ago

Above: Blaenau Ffestiniog in Victorian times. This is a remarkable photograph with much of interest. The pillars carry an Oakley Quarry slate line to the dressing mill. The line under the right 'arch' is the 1879 LNWR branch to Llandudno Junction. Beyond the pillars are the houses and smithy of Rhiwbryfdir, now lost beneath quarry waste. Below the wall by the buildings was the line to Oakley Quarry with a steep incline behind the right pillar. The two left hand pillars had their wooden supports replaced by stone for safety reasons. The pillar on the right remains without the wooden latticework. The other line in the foreground went to Llechwedd. The view towards the photographer was recreated in a painting by the late Edward Paget-Tomlinson, in the book Ffestiniog Railway Paintings by Philip J Hawkins, published by Landmark

Left: The railway arrived relatively late into North Wales but found a ready market for the movement of agricultural and mineral traffic, including animals which had been driven for centuries to English markets. This shows the Ffestiniog to Bala train leaving Blaenau Ffestiniog in 1883, the year the branch line was opened by the Great Western Railway

Right: Splitting and dressing slate in 1894 at Llechwedd. Dust from this process often brought on lung disease and an early death

Below: An inclined tramway at Dinorwic Quarry, Llanberis. The photo was taken in August 1958 and one of the incline cables may still be seen on the photograph. The small stretch of rail on the left hand side is particularly interesting and potentially much older than the other rails

Left: A huge underground chamber caused by the excavation of slate at Llechwedd, also taken in 1894

Below: Two rows of slate workers former cottages at Dinorwic in 1958

The enormous slate tips in North Wales indicate very well the extent of the mining and quarrying of slate in former days. Here are two views of the main production mills at Oakley (above) and Llechwedd (below) in 1894. Notice the huge timbers supporting the roof and giving a large uninterrupted production space. They were imported from Canada

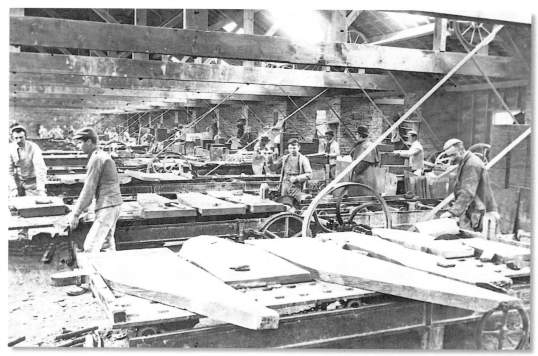

Beddgelert has a special charm appreciated by visitors and locals alike for centuries. Situated in a valley surrounded by magnificent scenery, this village has always been a popular watering 'hole'

This shows the small bridge and mill situated on the outskirts of Beddgelert. Some of the ruins of the building may still be seen when approaching from Nant Gwynant, east of the town

This is a familiar view of the Aberglaslyn Pass from the bridge, looking up towards Beddgelert. From the T-junction here, roads go off to Beddgelert, Portmadoc or Nantmor and on to Ffestiniog

A lovely view of a bygone scene which once would have been a daily sight at Portmadoc, (now Porthmadog). Some await a new cargo of slate, others are rigged and ready for another journey

Porthmadog harbour, c. 1880, showing the Oakley wharf (left) and the Greaves wharf (right)

The Britannia Bridge, Porthmadog, showing more slate wharves and sheds in 1894

Everything was loaded and unloaded by manual labour as may be seen in this interior view of the Greaves' storage shed on the quayside at Porthmadog

Masses of cut slates from Blaenau Ffestiniog awaiting transhipment. The slates arrived here on wagons brought down the Ffestiniog Railway. Two of their wagons may be seen on the line on the left side of the quay. All these slates await loading onto the barque moored alongside. Blaenau Ffestiniog slates were marketed worldwide under the strapline 'Best Portmadoc (sic) slates'

Two views of the crew of the *Evelyn* registered at Portmadoc (sic). Many boats were built in former times both here and at other small coastal ports – even on the beach at Porth Dinllaen

Criccieth Castle, another of the strongholds built by Edward I

Another scene of Criccieth showing initial development to the west of the castle

The spectacularly situated Harlech castle was built in the time of Edward I. When it was built it was on the coast, but it now looks out over fields, marshes and sand dunes to the sea, which is ½ mile away.

Pwllheli, with an early view of the harbour

The town gained popularity as a tourist destination and grew substantially as a result

Barmouth is situated at the mouth of the Afon Mawddach, surrounded by magnificent scenery on a beautiful estuary. It was once an important port and vessels sailed from here to The Continent and on into the Mediterranean

This scene shows the impressive railway bridge across the Afon Mawddach at Barmouth. It is 0.5miles in length and is constructed of wood, with the exception of the portion which spans the channel of the river. Here for 400 feet it is constructed of great iron girders supported on steel cylinders driven into the river bed

A lovely view of the Afon Mawddach. Was this a locally-built boat?

A busy day at Dolgellau Fair

Corwen on Market Day

Llangollen Bridge is regarded as one of the seven wonders of Wales. It is said to have been built in the reign of Henry I and incorporates four irregular pointed arches. It was widened as early as 1346 and again in 1873 as well as being lengthened to accommodate the railway. When this work was carried out, a stone was found in one of the arches bearing the date 1131 and the letters WS

Llangollen is situated on the River Dee. It occupies a site in a dramatically situated valley between two ranges of hills. The valley is 7miles of spectacular scenery and has been hugely popular since Victorian times. Castel Dinas is just visible on the top of the hill overlooking the town

This unusual scene shows a former cottage by the pool at the rear of Valle Crucis Abbey. This Cistercian Abbey was founded in 1201. There are extensive remains and a fine collection of medieval memorial sculptures

A pleasure craft on the Llangollen Canal

The Square, Ruthin is said to have more listed buildings than any other market town in North Wales and several delightful old buildings seen here remain

Ruthin Castle from the gardens. The hotel incorporates the castle ruins of which quite a lot survives, especially the walls

Left: Denbigh Castle, built by Henry de Lacy, Earl of Lincoln in the reign of Edward I. Much of the castle was slighted after the Civil War. The Entrance Gate was flanked by octagonal towers, now largely unrecognisable. This image is thought to be very old

Below: The High Street and Market Place, Denbigh

Rossett Mill, which still retains its grinding machinery and undershot waterwheel, is open to the public at certain times. This photograph dates from c. 1910. The mill was built in c. 1474 and was extended in 1661; the date appears on the front elevation

Rossett Station, with many farmers waiting to load their milk churns. This was a busy station in its heyday as the station was on the line from Shrewsbury to Birkenhead via Chester

The High Street, Holywell

The New Inn at Dyserth

The High Street, St Asaph

The Cathedral and bridge, St Asaph

Fun and games at the Marine Gardens, Rhyl

Rhyl Promenade and the short-lived Queen's Palace behind. It had a large theatre and ballroom but was destroyed by fire in 1907. It had a magnificent interior, which was all lost

Above: Ladies with their perambultors enjoying a day on the beach at Rhyl

Right: These performing actors had gathered a large crowd on The Promenade

Below: The pier shortly after completion and before the Promenade had been built. The pier was demolished in 1973

Above and right: Two views of the Pavilion at Rhyl. A Grand Pavilion had been built in 1891 at the entrance to the pier but was destroyed by fire in 1901. This Pavilion was built near to the Marine Gardens and had a theatre with a capacity of 1,153

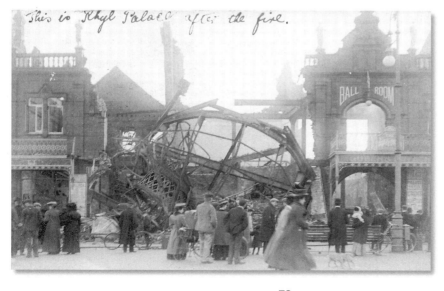

Left: All that was left of the lovely Queen's Palace after the fire in 1907

Two views of the main street, Pensarn

An excursion on a carriage and four close to Llanfair Talhaiarn

A very old view of the bridge at Llanfair Talhaiarn. Note the carriages and crowd on the bridge

Above and right: Rhuddlan Castle was the scene of the first parliament in Wales in 1284 following the death of the Welsh Prince Llewelyn ap Griffith in 1282. In 1284, the first English Prince of Wales was born at Caernarfon Castle. Rhuddlan was one of a chain of castles built by Edward I and was largely destroyed after the Civil War. Insurrection in Wales meant that the coastal castles to the west were left intact, e.g. Conwy and Caernarfon

Two old views of Abergele

W R Williams's grocers shop, Llandulas, with two coaches and what may be a dog cart at the rear

Raynes Quarry and limeworks, Llysfaen, near Colwyn Bay, 1917

Plough Terrace was alongside the turnpike at Colwyn Bay. Animals were driven along here to the nearby slaughterhouse, which was at the rear of Evan Jones' butcher's shop

The main road through Old Colwyn boasted 5 public houses within a quarter of a mile of each other. The Red Lion may be seen here on the right. It was originally known as the Union Arms. Note the transport taking visitors to the Fairy Glen; it is just passing the top of Beach Road on the left of the picture, which dates from c. 1905

Colwyn Bay pier, prior to its destruction by fire in 1922

Colwyn Bay Promenade from the pier. Construction of the prom ends in the mid-distance

Memories of four commercial premises in Colwyn Bay; Dicken's furniture shop (top) and Bryn Jones, fruiterers, (above). Dickens was described as being 'Artistic house furnishers', situated in Station Road. The store claimed to be the largest in North Wales and stocked everything. They were also Cabinet Makers, Removal Contractors and Funeral Directors! Braid Brothers' ran a motor garage (Opposite)

BEAUTIFUL BRITAIN

COLWYN BAY **BRAID BROS.**

AUTOMOBILE PALACE

SERVICE DEPOT:
DOUGLAS ROAD
COLWYN BAY

Telephone Nos.
464 and 465
Colwyn Bay

Telegraphic Address:
" Braids
Colwyn Bay "

Agents and Distributors for

VAUXHALL	HILLMAN
AUSTIN	LAGONDA
DAIMLER	ROVER
ARMSTRONG SIDDELEY	
CALTHORPE	F.I.A.T., Etc.

THE LARGEST DIRECT SUPPLIERS
OF AUTOMOBILES IN WALES

WE carry a stock of over 100 new and second-hand Cars. It will pay you to get in touch with us. Representatives sent any distance.

We will take modern Cars in part payment for any new Car. All enquiries receive prompt attention.

Any make of Car supplied.

This close up of Colwyn Bay pier was taken in 1923. The Urban District Council bought the pier in 1922 and built a new Pavilion, the former one having been destroyed by fire on 27th March 1922. The new one was completed by July 1923 and is seen here as a hive of activity

A procession passing the Post Office on Penrhyn Road, Colwyn Bay, c. 1904. The opening hours were from 7am to 9pm (weekdays) and 8am to 10am on Sundays, with three deliveries per day (one on Sunday)

Coaches preparing for excursions from outside the Metropole Hotel in Colwyn Bay. The hotel was built in 1898. During World War II, the Ministry of Food took possession of this and 37 other premises in the town

Nant-y-Ffynon, Llanelian, above Colwyn Bay

The Mountain View Hotel, Mochdre

This early view is across the fields towards the hill known as Bryn Euryn. On its lower slopes are the ruins of Llys Euryn, the dwelling place of Ednyfed Fychan, who was Chancellor to Llewelyn the Great and whose tombstone is in Llandrillo Church. Note the Little Orme in the background and the hay gathered in stooks

The Llandudno and Colwyn Bay Electric Railway Co's tram at Rhos. It opened in 1907 and closed in 1956

An early view to the west of Rhos Point. Rhos-on-Sea was described in the early 20th century as a 'curious little resort with a beach which benefits by not being overlooked by the railway'

An early view of Rhos-on-Sea pier, which was built in Douglas, Isle of Man, in 1869 and dismantled and rebuilt here in 1895. It was 1,500 ft long.

A busy scene looking towards Rhos Point and the pier

The building nearest the camera was the Rhos Abbey Hotel, demolished in 2001, viewed from the pier

Rhos Fynach. Known as the 'Marsh Farm of the Monks', it was one of the outlying farms attached to the abbey at Aberconwy. It not only served as a farm, but housed the monks whose duty it was to fish the nearby weir

Penrhyn Old Hall. This ancient house is situated between The Little Orme and Penrhyn. In 1561 it was the property of Robert Pugh, Sheriff of Caernarvonshire. Note the servants waiting for the owner to arrive. The building survives and is currently a hotel

One of Llandudno's first trams on the descent of Penrhyn Hill

Llandudno Promenade, which extends the whole length of the bay. Note the bathing huts, originally called bathing machines, numerous shelters and seats for the comfort of visitors. The Promenade was said to be so well lit by electricity at night that visitors could read whilst listening to the band

Llandudno Pier, which is 800 yards long. When this photograph was taken, the Pierhead could accommodate 2,000 people and an orchestra of 40 performers. The latter played every morning from Easter to October. Many sailings left the end of the pier bound especially for nearby ports such as Liverpool and the Isle of Man

Views of both of the bays of Llandudno showing only initial development. Today, development prevents a view of both shores

The description accompanying this view of Mostyn Street, Llandudno records that there were many fine shops and several imposing buildings, the principle of these being the Public Library, built with funds from Mr Andrew Carnegie, Mr John Walker and Lord Mostyn

This scene shows a volunteer recruitment day for a new Welsh Army, the brainchild of David Lloyd George, in Mostyn Street, Llandudno in 1914

A carriage and four outside St George's Hotel. This was Llandudno's first omnibus, pictured here in 1905. It ran between the hotel and Conwy railway station before the opening of Llandudno station

This tollgate was built on the junction of Llandudno Road and Llanrhos Road between Penrhyn Bay and Colwyn Bay and existed until 1921. Some years later in 1935, Llandudno Road was where Britain's first conviction for exceeding the 30 mph (48km) speed limit occurred

St George's Pier, taken in 1858, shortly after the first section was completed. The hut was where the entrance tickets were issued by Robert Jones, who is third from the left

This natural amphitheatre in a hollow on the Great Orme has been the site of open air entertainment for many years known as Happy Valley. Crowds would flank the grassy slopes to watch and listen to the daily shows. The theatre was constructed in 1933 to replace an earlier one destroyed by fire

The Station Hotel and Conwy Road, Llandudno Junction

Regular crossings of the River Conwy were made to and from Deganwy. Many of the passengers would have been staying in nearby Llandudno

Deganwy was a port constructed by the London and North Western Railway Company for the slate traffic from Blaenau Ffestiniog. Ferries would leave the pier and cross the mouth of the River Conwy for passengers wishing to visit Conwy or sail either down the coast to Penmaenmawr (at a cost of 2d/just under 1p) or go up the river to Trefriw

INDEX

A
Aberconwy 33, 87
Aberconwy House 33
Abergele 76
Aberglaslyn Pass 53
Afon Mawddach 60, 61

B
Bangor 2, 20, 21, 22, 31
Barmouth 60
Beaumaris 16, 17, 20
Beddgelert 4, 52, 53
Bettws-y-coed 45, 46
Britannia Bridge 14, 27, 54
Bryn Euryn 84

C
Caernarfon 4, 10, 11, 13, 20, 75
Capel Curig 47
Cattle fair 43
Colwyn Bay 23, 24, 77, 78, 79, 80,
  82, 83, 85, 92
Conwy 27, 28, 29, 30, 31, 32, 33,
  36, 41, 43, 75, 92, 94, 95
Conwy suspension bridge 27, 41
Corwen 62
Criccieth 57
Criccieth Castle 57

D
Deganwy 36, 94, 95
Denbigh 43, 66
Denbigh Castle 66
Dinorwic Quarry 49
Dolgellau Fair 61
drover 9
Dyserth 68

F
Felin Isaf 2, 18

G
George, David Lloyd 13, 91
Gladstone, W.E. 25
Gower's bridge 41

H
Happy Valley 93
Harlech castle 58
Holyhead 19, 24
Holywell 68

L
Llanberis 1, 6, 8, 9, 49
Llanberis Pass 9
Llandrillo Church 84
Llandudno 27, 36, 48, 85, 88, 89,
  90, 91, 92, 94
Llandudno Junction 27, 48, 94
Llandulas 77
Llanelian 4, 83
Llanfairfechan 26
Llanfair Talhaiarn 74
Llangefni 18
Llangollen Bridge 62
Llangollen Canal 64
Llanrwst 41, 43, 44
Llechwedd 48, 49, 50, 51
Llysfaen 77

M
Menai Bridge 2, 14, 15, 20
Miner's Bridge 47
Mochdre 84

O
Oakley Quarry 48

P
Paddle steamers 36
Penmaenmawr 23, 24, 25, 95
Penmon Priory 17
Penrhyn Bay 92

Penrhyn Castle 21
Penrhyn Hill 88
Penrhyn Old Hall 88
Pensarn 73
Pont-y-Pair 45
Porth Dinllaen 56
Porthmadog 5, 53, 54, 55
Portmadoc 53, 55, 56
Pwllheli 58

R
Rhiwbryfdir 48
Rhos-on-Sea pier 86
Rhos Fynach 87
Rhosneigr 2, 18
Rhos Point 85, 86
Rhuddlan Castle 75
Rhyl 70, 71, 72
River Llugwy 45
River Seiont 12
Rossett Mill 67
Rossett Station 2, 67
Ruthin 65

S
Snowdon 1, 4, 6, 7, 47
Snowdon Ranger Hotel 4
St Asaph 69

T
Tal-y-Cafn 30, 39, 40, 43
Telford, Thomas 27
Trefriw 30, 34, 35, 36, 37, 38, 41, 95
Tu-hwnt-i'r-bont 42

V
Valle Crucis Abbey 63
Victoria Hotel, Llanrwst 41

W
Water Bridge 27
Waterloo Bridge 45